CUTE CANDY

igloo

This is Candy. Isn't she cute? Everybody says that she is and they are all right.

Whatever she says, whatever she does, no one could do it more sweetly.

She doesn't even have to try to be nice. It's just the way she is. Friendly to everyone and everyone's friend.

People just smile when they see her.

Because she is so cute, she gets whatever she wants. If she were in the shop with her mum, she might say, "Would it be all right if I had a little sweetie, mummy?"

And her mum would just sigh happily and say, "Of course you can, you tiny little angel."

When it is her birthday, all the children in her class fight over who has got her the best card or her favourite present.

How wonderful it must be to be that cute. However. . .

At school, it was time to choose children to be in the school play. This year it was Little Red Riding Hood.

Candy put up her hand. "Please, Miss Fishlips, could I possibly be the Big Bad Wolf?"

The whole class went silent and then everyone burst out laughing.

All except William, that is. "That's not fair," he moaned. "I wanted to be the Wolf!"

Candy's face went as red as a strawberry and she started to cry. The tiniest, saddest cry in the whole wide world.

As soon as everyone all saw how sad she was, they stopped laughing and ran to find hankies for her to wipe her baby tears.

"OK, Candy," said her teacher. "Show me you can be nasty and I'll let you be the Wolf."

"I want to be the Wolf, though," said William. "Me, me, me, me, me!"

"Don't worry, William," said the teacher. "I'll find you a good part."

At playtime Candy asked Nancy, "don't you think I could be the Big Bad Wolf?"

"Never in a million years," Nancy said. "Your hair is far too long and fluffy."

"But *mummy* says it's beautiful!" she beamed. "I brush it one hundred times before I go to bed."

"And just look at your clothes," said Nancy. "They're all candyfloss pink. That isn't tough or frightening to anyone."

Nancy was right, of course. Candy was too cute for words. If she was going to be the Wolf, she needed help.

Candy asked Roger to show her how to make ugly faces, and how to stick out her tongue at grown-ups.

Tabitha rolled around on the floor crying at the top of her voice. "No one likes anyone who does this!" she screamed.

And Dave put his cap on Candy's head as he flew past on his skateboard.

"Hey, Candy," he shouted. "Now you look really cool."

By the end of school, Candy was ready to be mean and moody.

Wherever she went, Candy practiced being nasty.

One day at the shops, she crept up to a child in a pram. She snarled at him with her big, fierce teeth.

"Waaaah!" she whispered in her tiny little voice.

The toddler clapped his hands in joy. "Funny Wolfie," he giggled.

His Mum smiled at Candy. "How cute," she said. "Thank you for making him laugh."

Candy was not happy. "This is harder than it looks," she said to herself.

When Candy went for tea with Rebecca, she tried to be bad again.

"Would you like a sandwich, my dear?" asked her mother.

"You bet!" said Candy, gobbling them up like a hungry wolf. "And get me a drink, too!"

Then, to everyone's surprise, she did a great big burp.

Rebecca's mum got upset and took Candy home. She was sent straight to bed.

For the first time in her life, Candy had been really naughty.

"That's more like it," she thought. "I knew I could be bad."

But, soon, she was being sent to bed early every night.

After two more days, she wasn't even allowed out to play.

And, by the end of the week, no one was talking to her at all.

So, one morning at school, Candy went up to Miss Fishlips.

"Please, Miss," she said in her cutest voice. "I don't want to be the Big Bad Wolf anymore."

Her teacher knelt down beside her. "Oh, and why is that, Candy?"

"Because it's no fun being nasty all the time," she sniffled. "And no one likes me anymore."

So Miss Fishlips said that Candy didn't have to be the Wolf and everyone was happy. Especially William, because . . .

He really, really didn't want to be Little Red Riding Hood!

also available...

Rude Roger   Dirty Dermot   Pickin' Peter   Space Alien Spike   Silly Sydney   Nude Nigel

Shy Sophie   Cute Candy   Royal Rebecca   Grown-up Gabby   Terrible Twins   Show-off Sharon